JERICHO

A Celebration

First published 2022 by a 'Jericho Co-operative'

MY JERICHO   PAUL SOUTHOUSE ARCHITECTS   CHRIS ANDREWS PUBLICATIONS

Distributed by: Chris Andrews Publications Ltd, www.cap-ox.com Tel: 01865 723404

Illustrations by: Valerie Petts, Weimin He, Chris Andrews, W Lucy and Co,
Paul Southouse, Richard Wadey, Dominic Price, Mark Davies
Text by: Mark Davies with additions from John Mair
Edited by: Chris Andrews and John Mair
Design by: Zena Tuson
Printed by: Knockout Print

All rights reserved. No part of this publication may be reproduced, stored in a retrieval system, or transmitted, in any form or by any means, without prior permission of the copyright holders. The right of all contributors to be identified as authors of this work has been asserted by them in accordance with the Copyright, Designs and Patent Act 1988.

ISBN: 978-1-912584-74-1

Front Cover: St Barnabas Church and the Jericho Boatyard by Valerie Petts. Title Page: Walton Crescent. Half Title: Sunday music in Mount Place. Verso: The Oxford Canal at Jericho. Back Cover: Inside the Old Bookbinders Ale House.

JERICHO

4

CONTENTS

Foreword by Sir Philip Pullman

The Bohemian Republic of Jericho	06
Early Oxford and Today's Jericho	10
Introduction and Brief History	12
Jericho Today	22
The Oxford Canal	45
Churches and Colleges	52
Contemporary and Developing Jericho	68
Greater Jericho	70
Supporters and Map	74

Foreword by
Sir Philip Pullman

THE BOHEMIAN REPUBLIC OF JERICHO

Sir Philip Pullman on a place made to human measure.

In a little book I wrote a few years ago, *Lyra's Oxford*, I inserted a fake page from an imaginary guidebook to an Oxford in another world describing part of the Jericho in that other universe, and I called this part of the city "the coastline Oxford shares with Bohemia". Bohemia, of course, is the land where the bohemians live, which includes the Paris celebrated in Henri Murger's novel Scènes de la vie de Bohème, later the basis of Puccini's opera; and it's also the place on whose coast the ship was wrecked in Shakespeare's A Winter's Tale. Apparently there is a "real" Bohemia somewhere in the vicinity of the Czech Republic; but what does that matter? I believe there is a "real" Jericho too, somewhere even further away.

I have never lived in Jericho. But I count myself a citizen, and I bristle with indignation when this vivid and interesting part of the city is under siege. I lament the loss of every curious corner, I deplore the creeping invasion by the forces of Greedi-Build plc, I abominate the disappearance of old landmarks and familiar views.

Some years ago, the City Council decided to spare Jericho the sort of wholesale clearance that had taken place in St Ebbes. The result is that we can still walk through the little streets between Walton Street and the canal and feel that here is a place made to a human measure.

That's not to say that we should preserve everything as it always was, and never change at all. It was right, for example, some years ago, to clear a space for St Barnabas School; and the green space of the playground and the sound of children's voices

Lyra and barge.

are a valuable part of what Jericho is now. It's important to build doctors' surgeries and decent community centres. There was a time before St Barnabas Church rose in its Romanesque splendour; and no-one could say that Jericho would be better off without it. Jericho was better when it had Lucy's providing work for local people, with those crazy eagles guarding the gate; and there was a time before Lucy's too.

But as with all places that we cherish for their value to us as human beings, we have to be ready to defend them against those who can understand only the value of money. And unfortunately, people like that are in the ascendancy now; we live in a theocracy whose god is Profit. If Jesus were alive now, it wouldn't be ritualistic Sabbath-observance he'd be criticising, but the worship of money: "The market was made for man, and not man for the market," I think he'd say. And that remark would make him just as popular as the previous one did.

I used part of Jericho and the canal in my trilogy *His Dark Materials*, because people who lived and worked on the water, and the network of canals that spread through the whole kingdom, were useful for my story. (I hope that the gyptians and their life will be given full value in the forthcoming film).

But I didn't realise how much the present-day life of the canal was under threat until recently, when the boatyard business came to a head. I've always enjoyed walking along the canal, and looking at the activity – useful, human-scale, craft-based, untidy, interesting – in the boatyard, with the campanile of St Barnabas watching over it, and the calm water in front.

And the other day I was in the Ashmolean Museum and I saw a lovely painting by Canaletto showing the Brenta canal, near Venice. It's a scene of everyday activity: some elegantly dressed ladies and gentlemen out for a walk; one man fishing, another sitting on a pile of sacks of what might be corn or freshly ground flour; a lock; sunlight on the water; the spire of a church... Anyway, as I looked at it I was struck by the odd fact that only a few minutes away from the place where the picture hung, I could see exactly the same sort of thing, in real life.

And the painted one was catalogued and cherished and valued, and rightly so, because it's beautiful.

And the real one was going to be wiped out. All that useful social activity had to be done away with, because it was not making sufficient profit.

Isis Lock.

Well, we've gone wrong somehow in the way we live. Jericho is a place where it ought to be possible to maintain a working boatyard, to give a meaning and a focus to the life of the canal. If it does go, something irreplaceable will go with it. It would be a thousand pities if the only way of experiencing the sort of ordinary, age-old, decent, priceless human activity that the boatyard represents were to look at it in a painting on a museum wall, or to read about it in the pages of a novel.

First published in the *Jericho Echo* in 2006.
This is reproduced with the author's encouragement.

Sir Philip Pullman along with John Mair and Mark Davies addressing a My Jericho meeting in St Barnabas Church, February 2022.

EARLY OXFORD, AND TODAY'S JERICHO

Oxford in 1832.

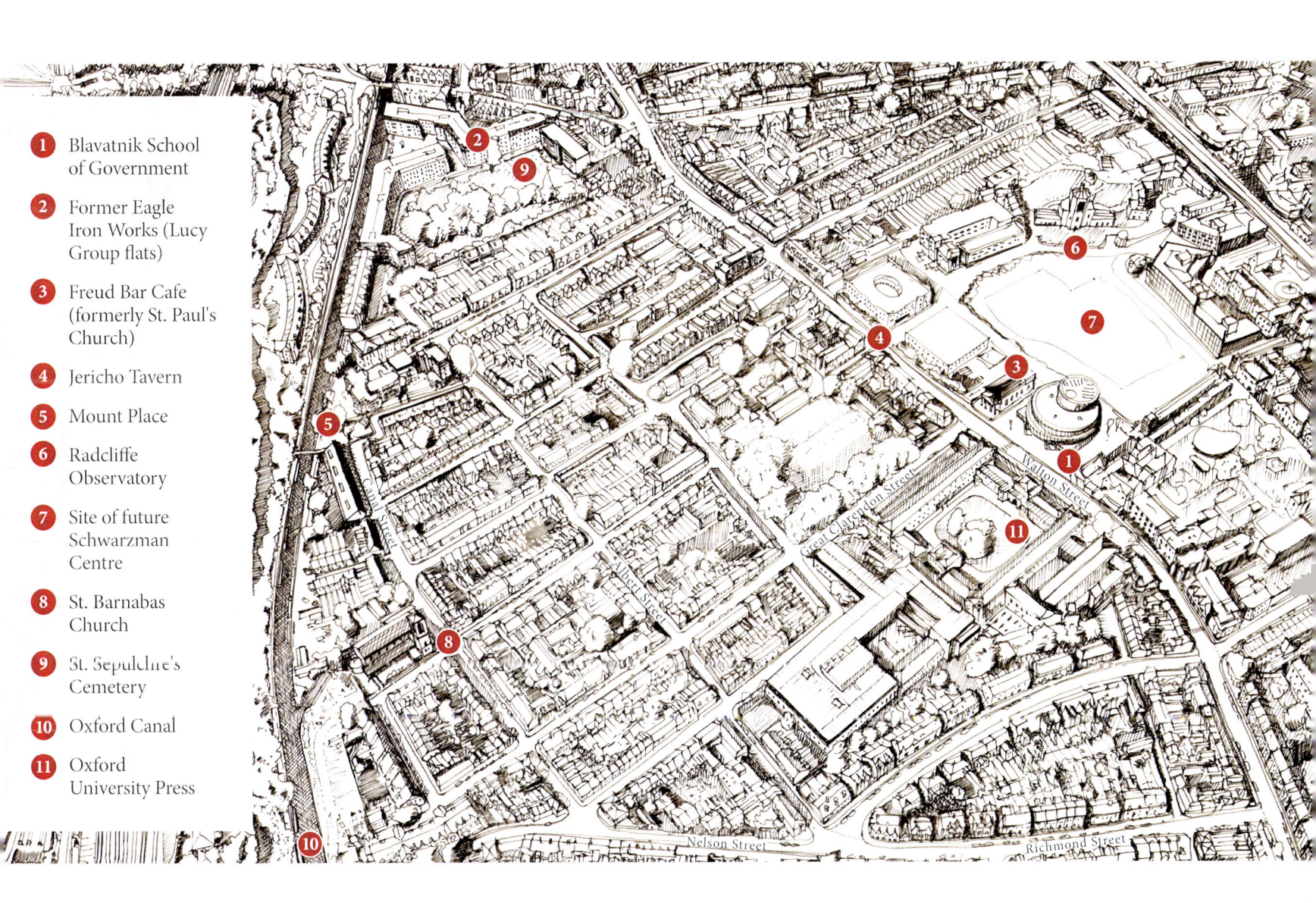

1. Blavatnik School of Government
2. Former Eagle Iron Works (Lucy Group flats)
3. Freud Bar Cafe (formerly St. Paul's Church)
4. Jericho Tavern
5. Mount Place
6. Radcliffe Observatory
7. Site of future Schwarzman Centre
8. St. Barnabas Church
9. St. Sepulchre's Cemetery
10. Oxford Canal
11. Oxford University Press

Jericho in 2022,.

INTRODUCTION AND BRIEF HISTORY

The earliest reference to the name 'Jericho' came in 1668. On 1 July of that year the Oxford diarist Anthony Wood spent sixpence at 'Jericho Gardens' in the company of a friend. The two men were probably supping ale that day in the grounds of the pub called Jericho House, and it seems somehow appropriate that this first mention of the Jericho name was in this context, given the future reputation the suburb would have for its proliferation of pubs and alehouses.

From Jericho House, sited near today's Jericho Tavern on Walton Street, Wood's view would have been of meadows sloping gently down towards the most easterly branch of the River Thames (today's Castle Mill Stream). These fields had once been part of the Norman baron Robert d'Ivri's Walton Manor; then the property of Osney Abbey, which designated the whole plot as 'Twentiacre'; and by the sixteenth century they were in private hands, owned by one Thomas Furse, a 'singing man' of Christ Church.

Furse, to continue the theme, was also a publican, licensed with his wife Elizabeth to keep an inn in the city, known first as Furres, then the Bear Inn. As a consequence their meadows – providing essential fodder as an adjunct to the success of a city centre enterprise which once had stabling for 30 horses – went under the name Great and Little Bear Meadows. The division was more or less along today's Jericho and Victor Streets.

The Furse family retained ownership of all of this meadowland until the end of the eighteenth century when the then head of the family, Peter Wellington Furse, was persuaded by the Oxford Canal Company to sell to them the westernmost strip. The acquisition of this land, bordering the Castle Mill Stream, at the time the main navigation channel of the River Thames, enabled the company to dig the penultimate section of its 90-mile waterway from the Midlands.

The canal brought huge change to Oxford and many opportunities. Locally the first step towards what would subsequently result in the complete urbanisation of the meadows between Worcester College and Walton Well Road was the establishment, by at least 1819, of a boat-building and repair dock at the north-western corner. It was run by the Ward family, who became wealthy and then politically influential as canal-based merchants and boat owners over three generations. The presence of this existing business, and probably an existing small ironworks, no doubt influenced William Carter to relocate his own ironworks from Summertown to an adjacent canal side site in 1825. Lucy's, ultimately, was the result.

1825 was also the year in which Furse, who lived in Devon, sold all of his remaining land. Most significantly he conveyed 3 acres, 2 roods, and 17 perches at the south-east corner to the University, the site chosen for the construction of their new Clarendon Press Building. It was sufficiently completed for the first books to be printed in 1830.

At the same time, bids were encouraged for the adjacent land. Thomas Mallam (an auctioneering name still present in Oxford) auctioned the first 42 lots on 4 July 1825, followed by another 30 lots later that year.

Two years later, 'all those two valuable meadows, containing about 16 acres, called the Bear Meads' were auctioned. It was the end of more than 250 years of the Furse family's ownership and the beginning of the transformation of the area over the next six decades into the narrow streets of compact houses which in essence have altered very little to the present day.

Many of Jericho's early residents found employment at the Press, or at the Jericho Iron and Brass Works, but there were also many small artisanal businesses and cottage industries, plus a public house or an alehouse on, it would seem, almost every corner.

The obvious architectural exception to the overall 'two-up, two-down' pattern is the dominating presence of St Barnabas Church, opened in 1869 as a result of the generosity of both the Ward family and of Thomas Combe, superintendent of the University Press. Arthur Blomfield, the architect, honoured Combe's instruction that 'not a penny was to be thrown away on external appearance or decoration'. A step inside, however, will reveal something rather different, with décor reflecting the church's role as a beacon of the nineteenth-century Oxford Movement, which inclined towards Roman Catholicism. Thomas Hardy (who had once been Blomfield's apprentice) captures this idea in his reference in *Jude the Obscure* to 'the church of ceremonies'.

The Canal Ferry.

From top to bottom: Walton Well dock. The Ferry, 1886. Jericho Fields c.1851.

A 'dangerously hospitable' neighbourhood

For almost a hundred years, Thomas Hardy was the most famous author to incorporate Jericho – or Beersheba, as he dubbed it – into a novel. Then along came Colin Dexter, only moderately well known when *The Dead of Jericho* was published in 1981, but considerably more so after it was filmed as the first ever TV episode of Morse in 1987. The novel starts with a brief overview of Jericho, within which, when comparing its typical small terraced houses to the looming presence of the Oxford University Press buildings, is the endearingly alliterative description of the latter as being 'bleakly out of place and rather lonely, like some dowager duchess at a discotheque'.

Few other authors in the interim had thought this working class suburb, worthy of much attention. John Betjeman did write a poem called *St Barnabas, Oxford* in 1945, albeit he appears unconvinced by the very grandeur of 'Byzantine St Barnabas' and the replacement of 'blue meadows we loved not enough' by the 'redden'd remorselessness' of Cardigan Street.

P. D. James, opened her 1986 novel *A Taste for Death* with the discovery of two bodies in the church, though she placed it in Paddington, next to the Grand Union Canal rather than by the Oxford one. James, who was born at 164 Kingston Road, regularly attended services at St Barnabas in later life. In her fictionally relocated church 'eight panels of the pulpit sported Pre-Raphaelite artwork': a subtle clue to the

St Barnabas Church.

importance of Jericho to artists such as John Everett Millais, Dante Gabriel Rossetti, and especially William Holman Hunt. The man behind this association was (with his wife Martha) Thomas Combe, who, as well as financing the building of St Barnabas, among many other local philanthropic gestures, also supported and accommodated these young artists at a time when their style of painting jarred with popular taste. Combe was also the man responsible for the first print-run of Lewis Carroll's *Alice's Adventures in Wonderland*, of which, on account of its perceived poor quality of printing, only a handful of (now priceless) copies survive.

So much for Jericho's architecture and artistic legacy. When it comes to the residents, A. N. Wilson's *The Healing Art* paints a positive 1970's scene: 'Once an industrial slum, the world of Jude the Obscure, it had blossomed in recent years into a socially various neighbourhood. Old residents rubbed along with students, chic professional people, a few dons, a few Jamaican families, some orientals.'

This convivial mix is decidedly at odds with the dubious earlier reputation of the evolving suburb. R. D. Blackmore established a precedent in *Cripps, the Carrier*, set in the formative years of the 1830s, when 'the place was lonely, dark, and villainous: foot-pads still abounded' and it was a 'dangerously hospitable' locale. The latter comment would appear to be a nod both to Jericho's numerous drinking establishments and to its reputation as a red-light district. Katy Darby expands on this theme in *The Whore's Asylum*, set among 'the seedy, maze like streets and ill-lit taverns of Jericho' in 1870s and 1880s, 'notorious as the haunt of drunkards, thieves, beggars, pedlars and the lowest sort of brazen female as ever lifted her petticoats'. Darby's *Jericho* is not all uniformly bad, however, and the Harcourt Arms, 'a squat modern brick public house with a swinging red sign' is identified as 'the sole vaguely reputable tavern in Jericho'!

From left to right: Illustration from *The Nursery Alice, 1890*. Thomas Combe 1860 by Charles Dodgson (Lewis Caroll). A 'dangerously hospitable' locale… One remainder of Jericho's numerous drinking establishments.

And so finally to Philip Pullman, for whom Jericho holds an especial appeal, and features often in the adventures of his heroine, Lyra. Even Sir Philip slips in an acknowledgment of Jericho's red-light reputation. This comes within the playful excerpt from a Baedeker guide included in *Lyra's Oxford*, a discrete short story which culminates in Juxon Street. In the section about the Fell Press (the Clarendon Press of Lyra's world) is the suggestion that 'Lolly Parsons, a notorious woman of easy virtue, operated a tavern in the very press itself during the hours of darkness, unknown to the pious owners'. Neither is Pullman unaware of Jericho's old reputation: he told the *Guardian* in 2002 that Lyra's Jericho is not far removed from the perceptions of the real one: 'raffish and jaunty altogether, with an air of horse-trading, minor crime, and a sort of fairground bohemianism'.

But it is the canal which features most prominently in Pullman's Jericho, where 'the wharves along the waterfront in Jericho were bright with gleaming harness and loud with the clop of hooves and clamour of bargaining'. He has been a consistent supporter of the long campaign to retain a boatyard in Jericho over the last two decades, sustaining the hope of a future Jericho waterfront along the lines of that experienced by Lyra. It is, after all, the canal which gives Jericho its greatest distinctiveness.

There is much more to Jericho than space allows here: important locations such as St Sepulchre's Cemetery, The Oxford Jewish Centre, Freud's wine bar, St Barnabas' predecessor as St Paul's: where Lewis Carroll preached his first Oxford sermon; of the brazenly glassy Blavatnik Building; and the imminent transformation of the Radcliffe Observatory Quarter beyond. Read on, though, for a glimpse of how 'the walls of Jericho' have changed over more than 200 years of vibrant, industrious and creative habitation.

Above: Juxon Street. Opposite: The Blavatnik and Somerville College buildings on Walton Street.

17

Jericho History Boards

In April 2022, Paul Southouse Architects, of Walton Street, with Mark Davies curated an exhibition of Jericho history at Lynrace Spirit. They provide the backbone for this book. The originals are on display in the Jericho community centre in Canal Street.

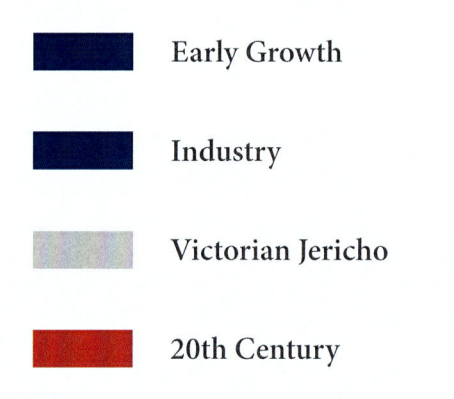

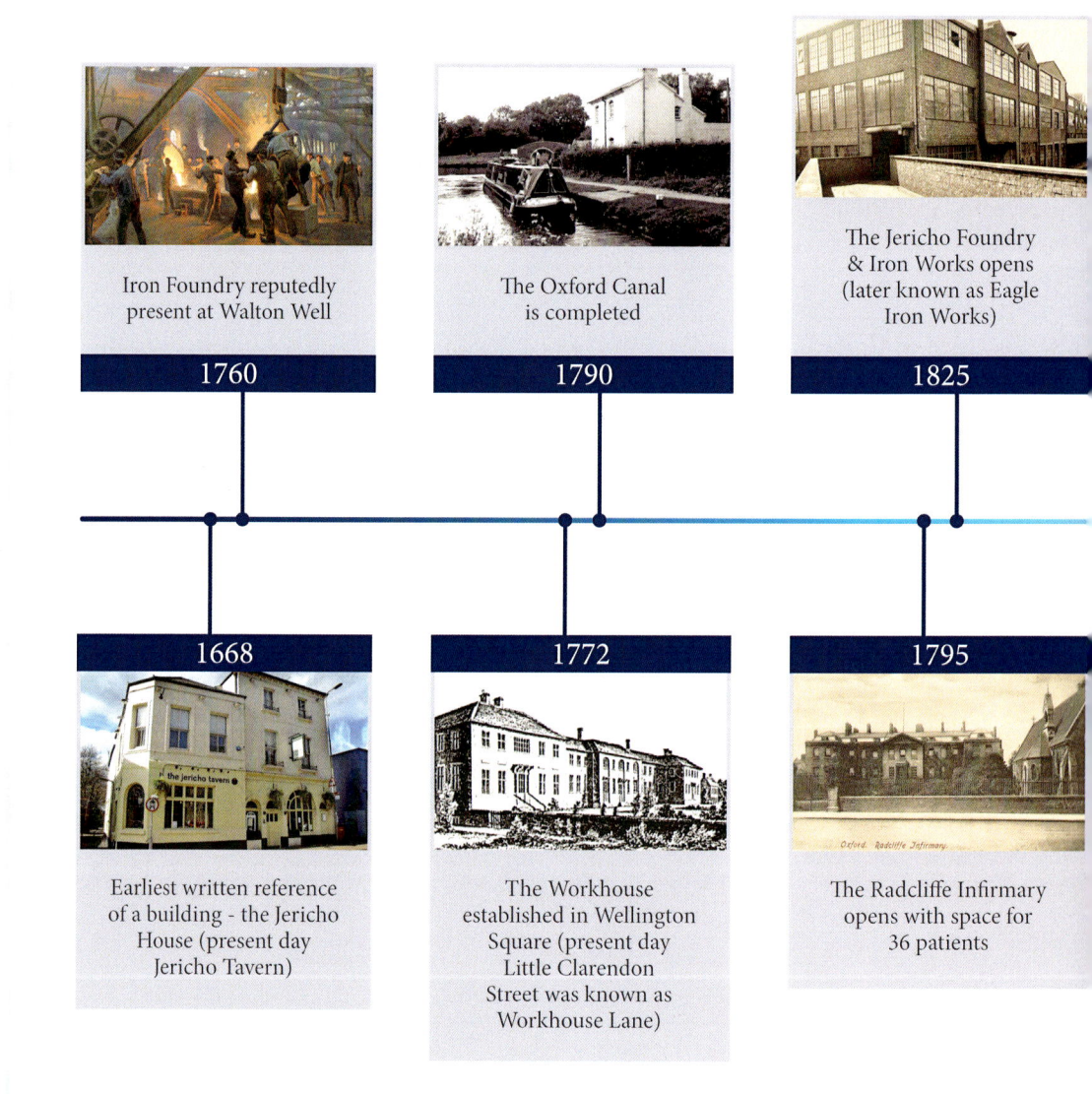

- Early Growth
- Industry
- Victorian Jericho
- 20th Century

1760 — Iron Foundry reputedly present at Walton Well

1790 — The Oxford Canal is completed

1825 — The Jericho Foundry & Iron Works opens (later known as Eagle Iron Works)

1668 — Earliest written reference of a building - the Jericho House (present day Jericho Tavern)

1772 — The Workhouse established in Wellington Square (present day Little Clarendon Street was known as Workhouse Lane)

1795 — The Radcliffe Infirmary opens with space for 36 patients

1760 Image from wikipedia.org. 1790 Image from oxfordcanalheritage.org. 1825 Image courtesy of Lucy Group.

Timeline

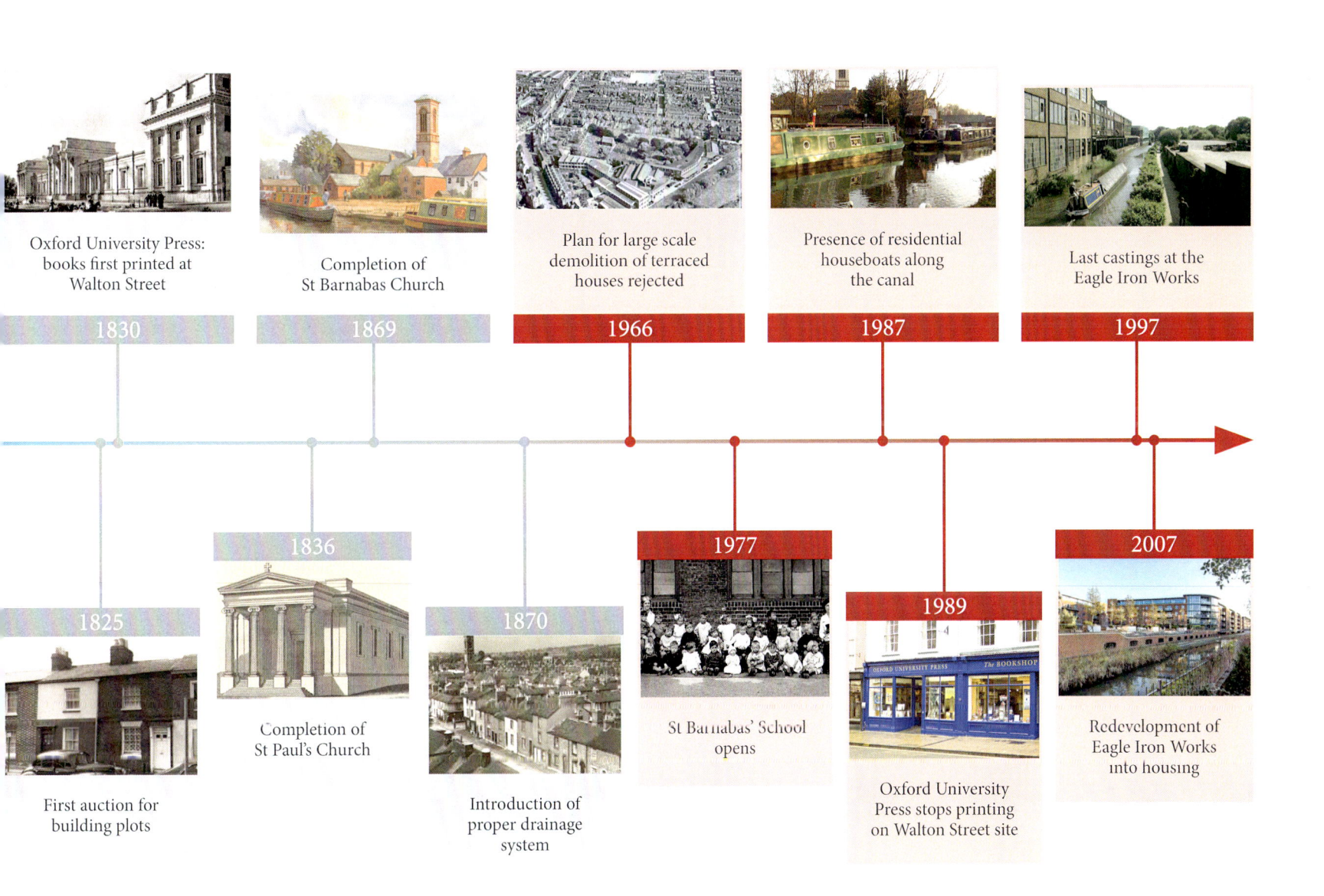

- **1825** — First auction for building plots
- **1830** — Oxford University Press: books first printed at Walton Street
- **1836** — Completion of St Paul's Church
- **1869** — Completion of St Barnabas Church
- **1870** — Introduction of proper drainage system
- **1966** — Plan for large scale demolition of terraced houses rejected
- **1977** — St Barnabas' School opens
- **1987** — Presence of residential houseboats along the canal
- **1989** — Oxford University Press stops printing on Walton Street site
- **1997** — Last castings at the Eagle Iron Works
- **2007** — Redevelopment of Eagle Iron Works into housing

1825 Image from andrewwhitehead.net. 1830 Image courtesy of Peter Stalker. 1870 Image from jerichocentre.org.uk. 1869 Image courtesy of Mark Davies. 1966 Image from britainfromabove.org.uk. 1987 Image from wikipedia.org.

Victorian Jericho and 20th century development

The growth of industry attracted a large number of workers to Jericho. The Oxford University Press and Eagle Ironworks became major employers in the local area – stimulating growth in housing and small businesses in the vicinity. Constraints on growth in the city centre meant that Jericho had great development potential.

Given that there were only two major landowners for the land around Jericho, development of the area was relatively uncomplicated. Land was organised into a basic grid pattern, radiating from Walton Street. Construction of the streets and workers' housing boomed between 1825 and 1870s to meet the demand. Growth was gradual however rather than the result of an overarching masterplan. Designed for workers of the Press and Ironworks, the majority of houses built around Jericho were compact terraced houses on narrow streets.

S. BARNABAS, OXFORD.

"Design a church to hold a thousand persons for as small a sum as possible and... to produce a dignified interior... and not a penny was to be thrown away on external appearance or decoration." *Description of St Barnabas Church, Arthur W. Blomfield, 1871.*

"Not many years ago, the meadows in this direction, which were flooded in the winter, were known as 'Wards Fields', the ground was then taken for gardens, and within the last three or four years these have given way to streets." *Jackson's Oxford Journal, 24 April 1868.*

Jericho is uniquely situated in Oxford, with its close proximity to the city centre to the south, canal to the west and Port Meadow to the north-west. Over the course of the 20th century, the area grew further into a thriving community and a highly desirable place to live.

During the 20th century however, Jericho still faced some challenges – including plans in the 1960s to demolish a large portion of the traditional housing stock and replace it with light industrial units, offices and new housing. A campaign by Jericho Residents' Association alongside local councillors (particularly the late Olive Gibbs) helped block the plans. Instead, only dilapidated housing was demolished but others were upgraded, as well as construction of social housing developments. The canal itself was also threatened with closure in the 1950s following the decline of its use for industrial transportation. The poet John Betjeman spoke out against the threat at a Town Hall meeting in 1955.

Jericho Aerial (1952)

The presence of residential narrowboats "positively increases the amenity value and security of the canal bank in our area. They turned an often dangerous towpath into an area integrated with Jericho". *Jericho Residents' Association in Oxford Times 11 June 1987.*

"It was about the time of the Horse Fair, and the canal basin was crowded with narrow boats, with traders and travellers, and the wharves along the waterfront in Jericho were bright with gleaming harnesses and loud with the clop of hooves and clamour of bargaining." *Northern Lights, Philip Pullman, 1995.*

Successful campaigners advocated leisure and recreation use to re-purpose the waterway that we enjoy today. Residential moorings for narrowboats were first established in the 1980s, further integrating the canal into the community.

JERICHO TODAY

This book uses the term 'Greater Jericho' to include The Radcliffe Observatory Quarter, William Lucy Way, Little Clarendon Street and Port Meadow as well as Worcester and Somerville Colleges. Jericho 'Proper' is a much smaller area bordered by the Canal, Walton Street, Richmond Road and Juxon Street. The 2011 census indicates there were then 1,400 residents in 695 households. The housing stock was 58% privately rented, 21% owner occupied and 20% council. Even in 2011, the area was mainly and increasingly middle class - 34% in higher managerial and professional jobs, 62% if you included lower managerial ones. Jericho residents are walkers and riders - 53% did not own a car then and there are now no bus services. The population changes regularly with more than a quarter of residents being students, mainly at Oxford University.

The Blavatnik and the Oxford University Press on Walton Street.

Radcliffe Observatory Quarter: The Old Radcliffe Infirmary and the Radcliffe Observatory.

The Streets and the Pubs and the People

Jericho is structured on a grid pattern, as Oxford's earliest planned suburb. It is defined by Walton Street, Juxon Street, the Canal, and Nelson Street (joined by Richmond Road). The photographs on the following pages provide glimpses of these thoroughfares, plus many others within Jericho proper, and an outline of the origin of some of their names may be helpful.

Walton Street is named after the manor of Walton, within which the area destined to become Jericho lay at the time of the Domesday Book in 1086, when it was possessed by Roger d'Ivri. The name is thought to mean literally 'homestead by the wall' i.e. outside the city. The Walton Street name has been used since 1772. The well of Walton was originally one of several springs which emerged from the gravel terrace - formed in the Ice Age - along which Walton Street runs. It is commemorated by a drinking fountain presented by Alderman William Ward at the junction of Walton Well Road and Longworth Road, close to the Ward family's canal dock.

Canal Street was in use by 1868, despite the 1876 Ordnance Survey map still labelling the area 'liable to floods'. Combe Road (named after the 19th century University Press printer and philanthropist, Thomas Combe) provides access from Canal Street to the canal. It was formerly named Ferry Road on account of the ferry which operated from June 1868 until the Mount Place footbridge made it redundant in 1972.

The houses adjacent to the boatyard were the setting for the first Inspector Morse TV film 'The Dead of Jericho', made for ITV in 1987.

A tallow factory once occupied the area now called Mount Place. It operated from at least February 1869, under the proprietorship of Charles James Harrison and John Butler Lucas, who resisted an 1899 petition signed by more than one hundred people complaining of the 'abominable nuisance'. The enterprise finally closed just before World War One. Today the location has been restored, planted by Greening Jericho, to become a quiet, canal side space which is also suitable for community events like 'Lazy Sundays', a music and beer festival held in the summer months.

Victor Street and Albert Street were named after Prince Albert Victor Christian Edward (1864–92), the oldest son of Edward VII. With Jericho Street, Victor Street marks the approximate division between Great and Little Bear Meadows (south and north of it respectively).

Other noteworthy names reflect St John's College's former ownership: Cranham Street is named after a St John's College living at Cranham in Gloucestershire, acquired in 1827, when the development of Jericho was just beginning, and Juxon Street commemorates William Juxon, President of St John's College between 1621 and 1633.

Nelson Street and Wellington Street were both named in the 1860s, after Horatio Nelson (1758-1805) and Arthur Wellesley, the Duke of Wellington (1769–1852) respectively, although the latter name also has (presumably unintentional) echoes of Peter Wellington Furse, the vendor of the meadows which once constituted this part of Jericho. As mentioned elsewhere, Little and Great Clarendon Streets are named after the Earl of Clarendon (1609–1674), a former Chancellor of the University and one of its greatest benefactors.

Finally, Hart Street is named after Horace Hart, the chief University Press printer from 1883 to 1915, and the last to live within the Press itself. Hart published the definitive, internationally recognised style guide for compositors, '*Hart's Rules*'.

Above: Ward's drinking fountain. Below: Juxon Street joining Walton Street with Brasserie Blanc on the corner.

Walton Street

The Jericho Café in Walton Street is a community hub. Today it is one of the many coffee shops in the area. US President Bill Clinton, a Rhodes Scholar from 1968-70, who lived at 46 Leckford Road, was a habitue. His daughter Chelsea followed him to Oxford to undertake a DPhil in 2001. When Bill, Hillary and Chelsea celebrated her doctorate at the Jericho Café with tea in 2020, the US Secret Service clogged up most of Walton Street!

The Phoenix Picture House, (formerly the Scala) was named the North Oxford Kinema when it opened in 1913.

27

Clockwise: Juxon Street and the Lucy 'Eagle' Works gates, Mount Street, Juxon Street and Mount Place.

29

Jericho's Pubs

Doors still open:

The Harcourt Arms has operated since at least 1869, but the present building dates from 1938. It is named after the wealthy and influential Harcourt family, of Nuneham Courtenay and Stanton Harcourt, but presumably especially Sir William Harcourt, Oxford MP from 1868 to 1880. The pub features in Katy Darby's Victorian novel, *The Whore's Asylum*, as 'the sole vaguely reputable tavern in Jericho'. Some students researching an Oxford Guidebook in 1980 wrote: 'They were not pleased to see us here. In fact, if looks could kill, there might have been no pub guide!'

Jericho Tavern, a hospitality venue has existed on this approximate site since the earliest known reference to the name 'Jericho', in 1668. Known at that time as Jericho House or Gardens, the current building dates from the 1860s, and has a proud tradition as a music venue. Oxford's most famous musical export, Radiohead, played one of their first ever gigs here in 1987 where they were billed as 'On a Friday'. Supergrass and many others including Mumford and Sons, The Falling Leaves and Foals have appeared at the Tavern since. An enlightened, but short-lived, women-only bar was trialled upstairs in 1984.

Jude the Obscure was originally called The Prince of Wales when opened in 1871. The name was changed in 1995, reflecting the local associations with Thomas Hardy's novel.

The Old Bookbinders Ale House, formerly Bookbinders' Arms, is referenced in Colin Dexter's *The Dead of Jericho* (1981), but as The Printer's Devil, a name given to apprentices in the printing trade, who often emerged from cleaning or adjusting the presses covered in black ink. The pub has been operating from at least 1869.

Rickety Press, formerly the Radcliffe Arms, was built 1872, named after the wealthy physician John Radcliffe (1652–1724), as too the nearby Infirmary and Observatory.

The Victoria was built in 1839, much earlier than the other remaining public houses of Jericho, and no doubt benefited from the thirsty workers of the University Press and still more the convenient and dehydrating ironworks. The University Writers' Club met here after World War Two, and the comedian Dudley Moore is said to have enjoyed playing the pub's piano.

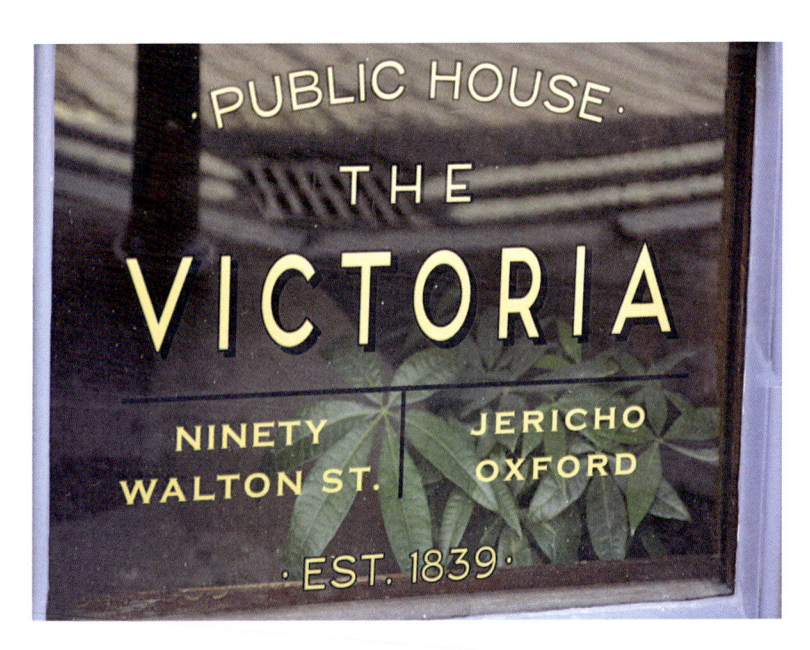

Pubs on which 'Time!' has been called, with their date of construction:

Bakers Arms, Albert Street, 1871; Bird in Hand, King Street, since at least 1880, closed 1925; Carpenter's Arms, Nelson Street, 1871 (once reputed to be haunted by a monk, and a favourite of Somerville College student Margaret Thatcher); Crown, Canal Street, converted from a cottage in the 1870s, and said to be a favourite with passing boat people; Duke of Wellington, Wellington Street, 1884; Fountain, Cardigan Street, circa 1872; closed 1976, to make way for the construction of the current school; Globe Inn, Cranham Street, 1861 originally, but demolished and rebuilt in 1932; New Inn, Nelson Street, since at least 1871, with stables at the rear, unusually for Jericho; Plough & Anchor, Great Clarendon Street, since at least 1831, and therefore Jericho's earliest, closed 1922; Union, Union Street (now Hart Street), circa 1888, closed 1924.

Above: The Victoria. Below: Site of the Globe pub.

The Old Bookbinders, Canal Street. The Rickety Press, Cranham Street. Lynrace and Branca on Walton Street.

Jude the Obscure, inside and out. Harcourt Arms sign, Al Shamir, the Lebanese restaurant, above the restaurant is a hotel, when the building caught fire guests were evacuated and slept on the floor of the synagogue opposite. Great detente!

Music and the Area

The Jericho Tavern and drummer, canal side concert. Jericho Community Choir.

Traders and Shops

Architectural Styles and Development

Jericho represents the Georgian and Victorian industrial and residential expansion of the City of Oxford into the surrounding countryside. It is an area of working class and artisan housing that has developed a unique character interspersed with landmark buildings of significant architectural importance.

Residential architecture is simple but embellished with architectural detailing often unique to an individual property or property group.

Streetscapes are generally typified by a uniformity of building line, roofscape, fenestration and materials, though the examples to the left, within 100m of each other on the same side of Walton Crescent show marked diversity.

Opposite: Canal Street looking to St Barnabas with the old Auto Works.

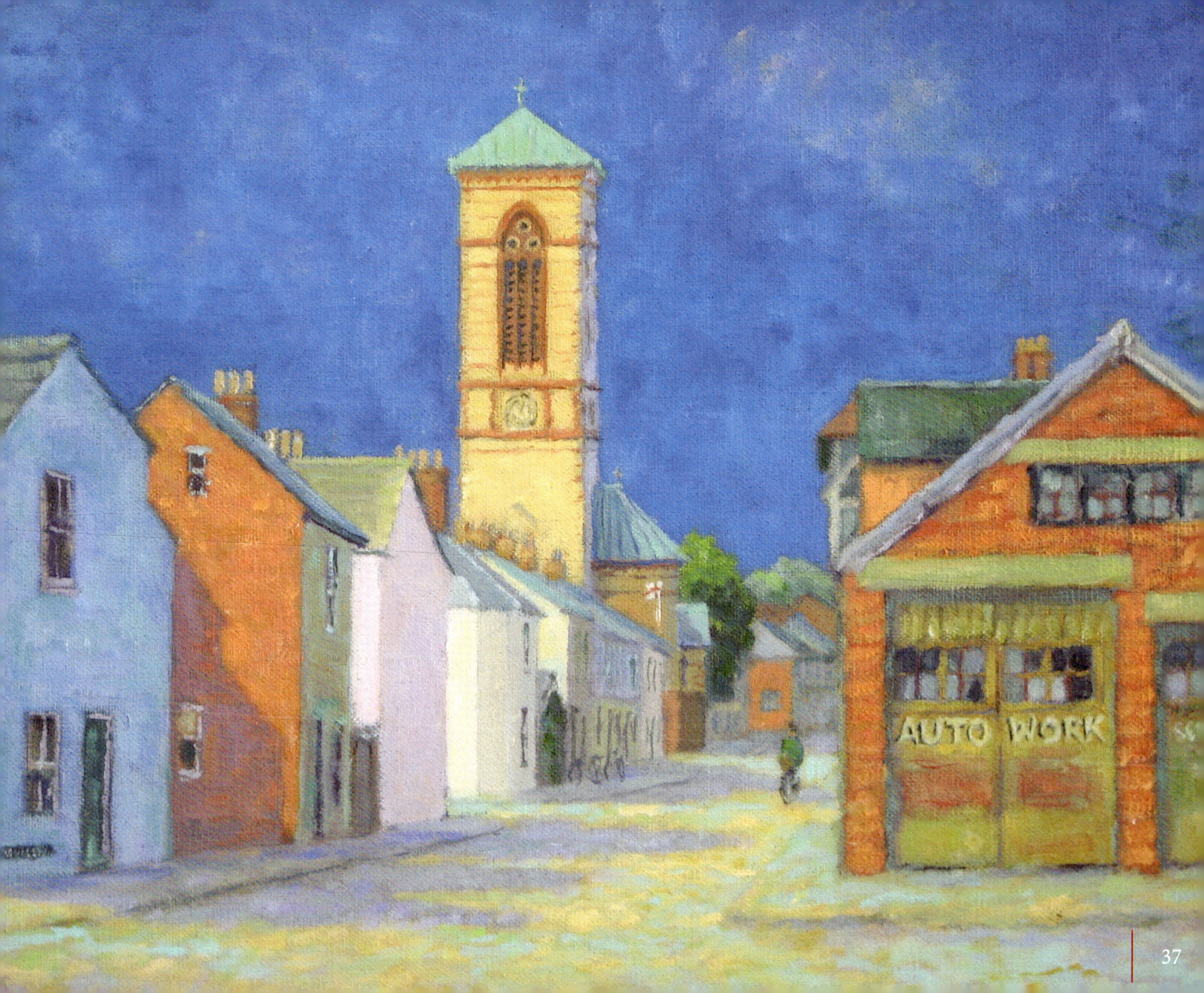
AUTO WORK

Industry - OUP

Jericho grew up around two big factories and employers; the Lucy Works in Walton Well Road and the Oxford University Press (OUP) in Walton Street. OUP is a department of the University of Oxford and was built between 1826 and 1832 on land first purchased from the Rev. Peter Wellington Furse, owner of all the meadowland now occupied by modern-day Jericho. Printing began in 1830 but ceased in 2021, though publishing work continues. The buildings still dominate a huge area bounded by Walton and Great Clarendon Streets. 'The Press' used to be intimately involved in the community, but is less so now. Leading lights linking the two include Thomas and Martha Combe.

Above: OUP in the 1830s and present day. Opposite: Inside the glass atrium main entrance on Great Clarendon Street.

39

Lucy Group

Industrial Jericho was Lucy's, and The Press. These two giants straddled and gave work and identity to the community. Today, Lucy's as a factory has gone, replaced by a rather attractive semi-gated community. This was home to P. D. James, the writer, and is today home to professionals and students alike. The buildings are on the site of the former Jericho 'Eagle Iron & Brass Foundry', later known as 'Lucy's'. A foundry operated here with certainty from 1825, and quite possibly, on a small scale for many decades previously. Immediately adjacent, where Walton Well Road crosses the canal, a boat building dock owned by the Ward family operated for most of the 19th century.

Lucy's Walton Well Road entrance with pictures from the c.1960s.

41

Lucy's has written its own history on the informative hoardings outside the construction site at its mixed-use redevelopment of St Paul's House on Walton Street. The project will be completed in spring 2023.

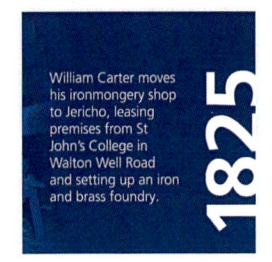

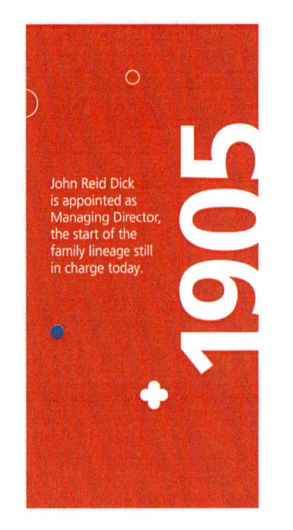

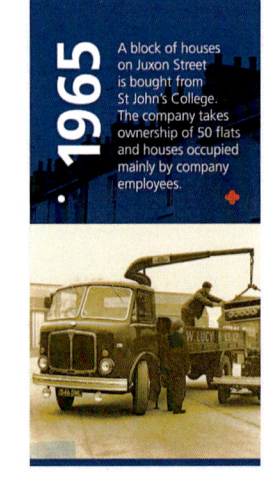

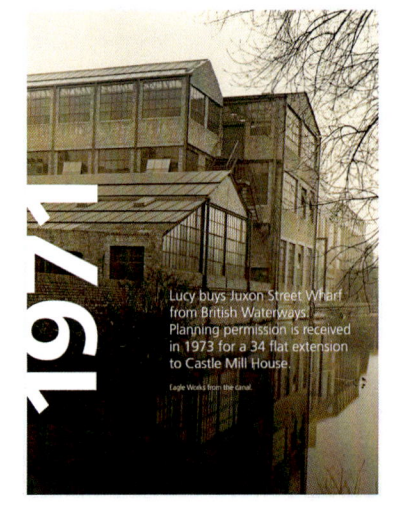

1825 — William Carter moves his ironmongery shop to Jericho, leasing premises from St John's College in Walton Well Road and setting up an iron and brass foundry.

1864 — William Lucy joins the leadership after 10 years at the company, and the name changes to Grafton and Lucy. *The eponymous William Lucy - a rare picture that came from his great granddaughter.*

1905 — John Reid Dick is appointed as Managing Director, the start of the family lineage still in charge today.

WW1 & WW2 — Lucy supports the war effort, making bomb casings and shells. *Aerial photograph, highlighting area occupied by the factory and the company bridge over the canal.*

1965 — A block of houses on Juxon Street is bought from St John's College. The company takes ownership of 50 flats and houses occupied mainly by company employees.

1971 — Lucy buys Juxon Street Wharf from British Waterways. Planning permission is received in 1973 for a 34 flat extension to Castle Mill House. *Eagle Works from the canal.*

1989 — The Walton Meadow site is sold and redeveloped into what is now Waterside.

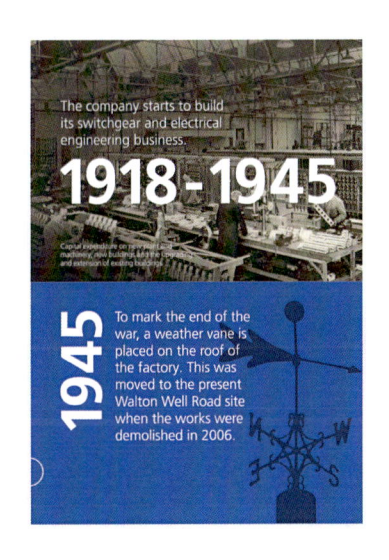

1918-1945

The company starts to build its switchgear and electrical engineering business.

Capital expenditure on new plant and machinery, new buildings and the forwards and extension of existing buildings.

1945

To mark the end of the war, a weather vane is placed on the roof of the factory. This was moved to the present Walton Well Road site when the works were demolished in 2006.

1954

Lucy buys the freehold of the Eagle Ironworks site from St John's College.

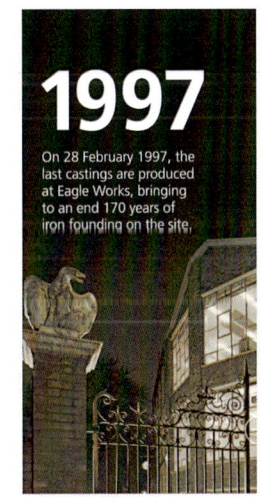

1997

On 28 February 1997, the last castings are produced at Eagle Works, bringing to an end 170 years of iron founding on the site.

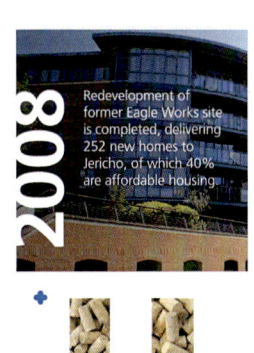

2008

Redevelopment of former Eagle Works site is completed, delivering 252 new homes to Jericho, of which 40% are affordable housing.

2021

Work begins on the development of this building - St Pauls House, the former Jericho health centre.

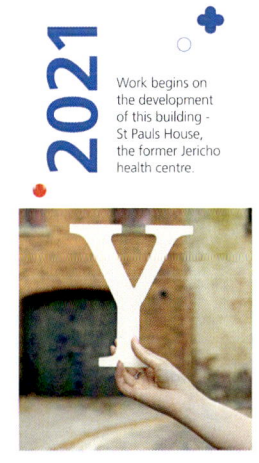

43

44 | The factory site from the canal, 1980s and present day.

THE OXFORD CANAL

THE OXFORD CANAL

Construction of the Oxford Canal began near Coventry in 1769, to facilitate the movement of coal and manufactured goods from Britain's expanding industrial heartland of the Midlands. Twenty years later the approximately 90-mile canal was completed to Oxford, the final stretch necessitating the purchase of meadowland adjacent to what would become the suburb of Jericho in the following century, and also a strip of Worcester College's riverside land. The first boats entered the city on 1st January 1790. For a city distant from both the nearest coalmine and port, the significance of accessibility to cheap and reliable sources of coal was huge, and the economic and social impact immediate and long-lasting.

The canal had a national significance as one of four original trunk canals which linked the major ports of Hull, Liverpool, Bristol and London, the latter being reached via Isis Lock, which began its colourful, sometimes macabre, history with construction by prisoners in the 1790s. By the 1920s, with trade steadily diminishing, the Oxford Canal Company decided to sell its city-centre terminus on the basis of 'having ample alternative accommodation in the Jericho Wharves for delivering and stacking of all goods carried on the Canal'.

The canal, St Barnabas and the 'Northern Lights'.

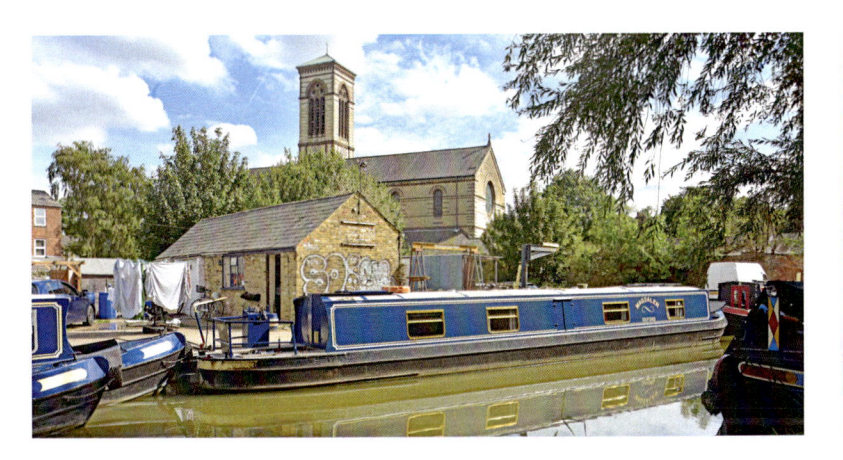

College Cruisers is a thriving boat hire and servicing business at the Jericho canal side, their boats are named after Oxford Colleges. The adjoining boatyard site still awaits redevelopment.

College Cruisers. 47

The monthly summer music festival with musicians performing on a floating stage boat on the canal.

Nuffield College spire from Isis Lock with Worcester College bounding the canal on the left and the Thames to the right (pictured in 1982).

The lock, colloquially known until recently as Louse Lock, is the access point for boats navigating between the River Thames and Oxford Canal.

Isis Lock summer and winter.

Built in 1796 as a wide barge lock, the narrowed current structure dates from 1844. Photos from 2022 and 1982.

CHURCHES AND COLLEGES

St Barnabas Church in Cardigan Street was designed by Sir Arthur Blomfield, whose instruction from Thomas Combe of OUP, who paid for the construction, was that 'not a penny was to be thrown away on external appearance or decoration'. A focus for the High Anglican Oxford Movement when it was built in 1869, the church features in Thomas Hardy's *Jude the Obscure* as the 'church of ceremonies'. P. D. James, who lived nearby and worshipped at the church, transplanted it to Paddington in *A Taste for Death* and in the Oxford of Philip Pullman's Lyra, it becomes the church of 'St Barnabas the Chymist'.

The former St Barnabas Church of England School in Great Clarendon Street was built initially for boys in 1856 but was closed and converted to housing in 1979. A school building for girls and infants erected later to the rear was demolished at the same time. The school is now in Hart Street.

The synagogue, (The Oxford Jewish Centre), in Richmond Road was built in 1973, replacing a hall which had been utilised by Oxford's Jewish population since 1893. The Centre is one of the few in the UK which encompasses all the Jewish religious denominations.

The Baptist Chapel, Albert Street, built 1881 was in some disrepair until revived by American Baptist evangelists in recent years.

St Paul's Church, Walton Street was built in 1835, to cater for the rapidly growing population of Jericho. It is Oxford's only Greek Revival church, and the first in Oxford at which Charles Dodgson (Lewis Carroll) reluctantly preached a sermon. It was deconsecrated in 1964 and Freud's, a wine bar, now occupies the site.

St Sepulchre's Cemetery on Walton Street was consecrated in 1848 as one of several outlying sites selected to alleviate pressure on the city's central graveyards. As well as being the burial ground for local churches, six colleges, namely Balliol, Exeter, Jesus, St John's, Trinity and Worcester, made use of the cemetery when they were no longer permitted to bury their dead under their chapels; and when Keble was built in 1868, it was included. The Cemetery was closed for new burials in 1945. There are many notable graves which are well documented on the cemetery website and the site is well looked after by dedicated volunteers.

St Barnabas Church

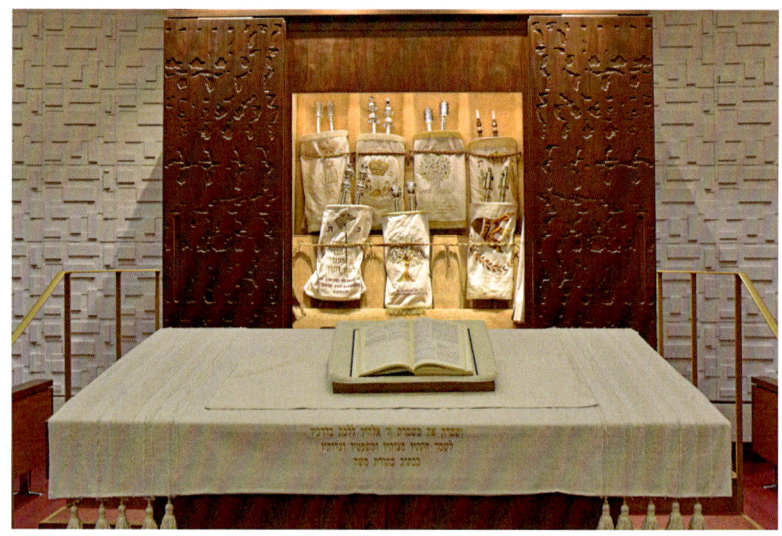

54 Former St Barnabas Church of England School, Great Clarendon Street. Inside the synagogue in Richmond Road. At the Baptist Chapel, Albert Street.

St Paul's Church, now Freud's Wine Bar

Peace, by Charles Kempe (1888-94) inside St Paul's/Freuds. It shows the ceremony of the consecration of the firstborn son, with Simeon taking Jesus into his arms. Beneath is The Conversion of Saul of Tarsus.

55

| St Sepulchre's Cemetery

"The gloomiest and most enthralling of the Oxford burial places" *(Jan Morris Oxford, 1965)*.
The cemetery is an oasis of wildlife in the close urban housing of Jericho. St Sepulchre's environment is managed by a gardening group of local volunteers.

Worcester College

There has been an institution of learning on this site since 1283, originally as Gloucester College, it was re-founded in 1714 as Worcester College after a benefaction from Sir Thomas Cookes, a baronet of Worcestershire.

Between 1720 and 1864 four major architects, namely Hawksmoor, Wyatt, Keene and Burges, designed all the central college buildings. The newest building is the Sultan Nazrin Shah Centre, comprising an auditorium, meeting rooms and dance studio. Designed by Niall McLaughlin, it was donated by Honorary Fellow HRH Sultan Nazrin Shah and opened in 2017 by the Duchess of Cornwall.

The extensive grounds of 25 acres include beautiful gardens, a lake and sports fields.

Main entrance and the lake.

Somerville College

Founded in 1879 by the Association for the Education of Women in Oxford but was only given full college status in 1959. Formerly for women only it is now a mixed college. Notable college alumna include Nobel Prize wining chemist Dorothy Hodgkin, politicians Shirley Williams, Margaret Thatcher and Indira Gandhi, authors Iris Murdoch and Dorothy L Sayers, Britain's first female ambassador Anne Warburton and soprano Emma Kirkby. Mrs Thatcher lived for a while at 12 Richmond Road in Jericho with what she called 'three red-hot communists'.

The Library and a view through to the Radcliffe Quarter. Opposite: the gardens looking towards Walton Street buildings.

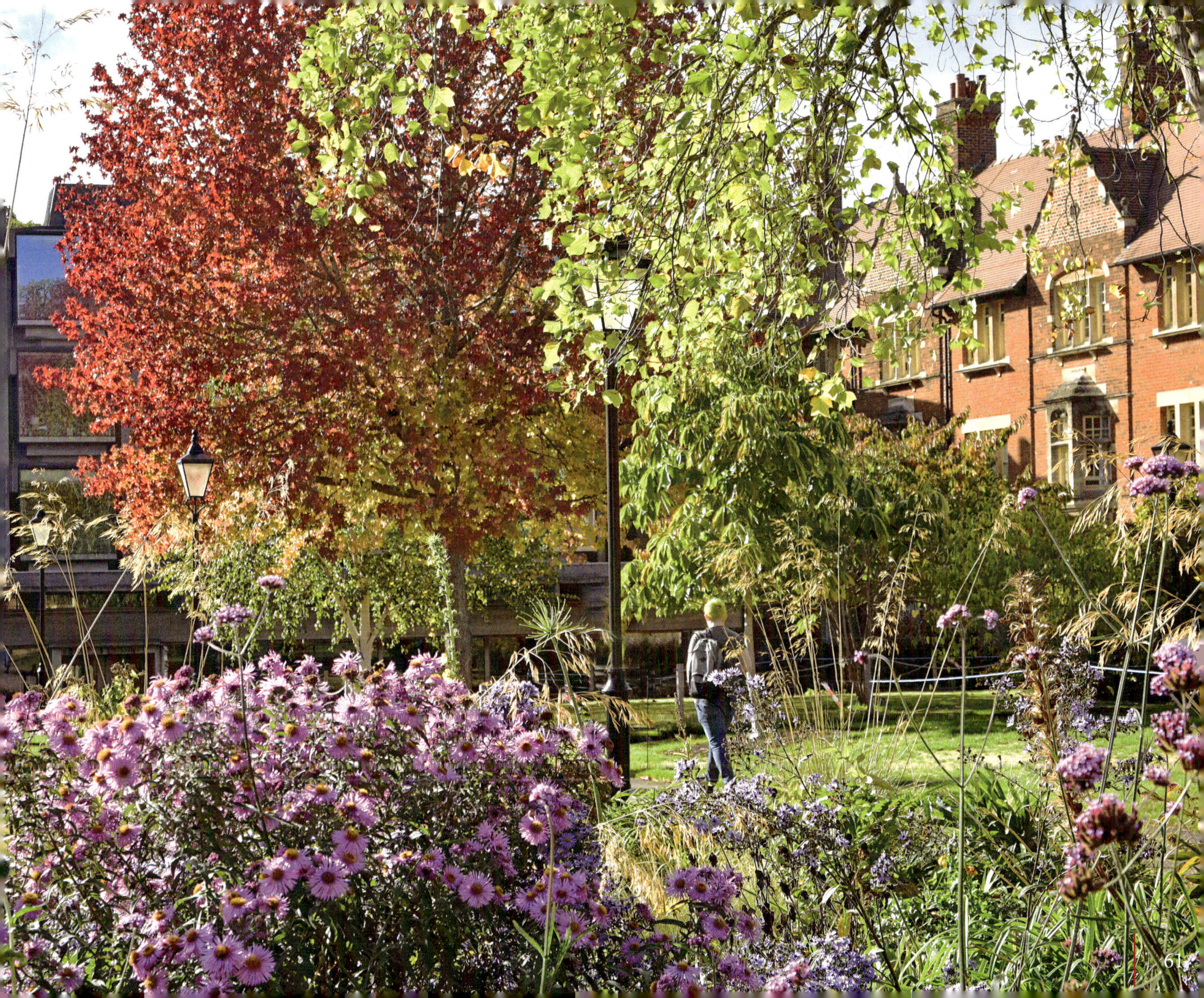

The Blavatnik School of Government

One of the University of Oxford's newest departments. Founded in 2010 it is housed in a distinctive circular building by Herzog and de Meuron on Walton Street. The School educates leaders and potential leaders from all over the world on short and long courses.

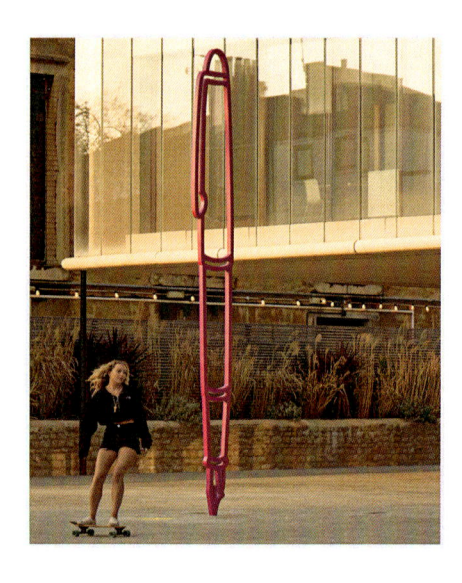

Michael Craig-Martin's sculpture *Fountain Pen*, 2019, was commissioned by the Blavatnik School to celebrate the Radcliffe Observatory Quarter and 'enliven' the local environment.

63

64 These lively illustrations show construction work on The Blavatnik by the University Artist in Residence, Weimin He.

The Radcliffe Infirmary and Quarter

The most interesting major Jericho development in the last two decades has been the closing down and demolition of the Radcliffe Infirmary site, and its subsequent development by the University of Oxford. Now known as the ROQ (Radcliffe Observatory Quarter), it contains the Blavatnik School of Government, the new Jericho Health Centre, the Mathematical Institute and the Humanities Department. The largest project, due to open in 2025 is the Schwarzman Centre for the Humanities, at the heart of the quarter.

Its many facilities, for both University and public use, will include a 500-seat concert hall and 250-seat auditorium

The original Infirmary, now part of the university's Mathematical Institute, was opened in 1770, using the bequest of Dr John Radcliffe (1652-1714). Dependent on public subscriptions originally, the Infirmary hosted a number of progressive treatments over the years, and it was there that the unique effectiveness of penicillin was demonstrated.

The Radcliffe Infirmary and St Luke's Chapel.

The beautifully restored Radcliffe Infirmary, St Luke's Chapel and the fountain depicting Triton.

The Radcliffe Observatory, constructed between 1772 and 1794, also using the bequest of Dr John Radcliffe, was a meteorological station, and clearly influenced the street pattern of Jericho, since the orientation of Cardigan Street provides a view line directly aligned to the Tower of Winds from St Barnabas Church. It ceased being used for astronomy in 1935, and is now part of Green Templeton College.

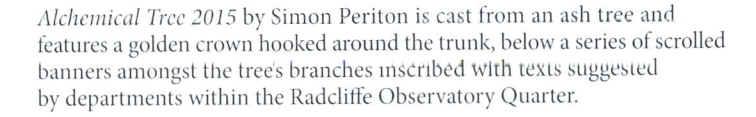

Alchemical Tree 2015 by Simon Periton is cast from an ash tree and features a golden crown hooked around the trunk, below a series of scrolled banners amongst the tree's branches inscribed with texts suggested by departments within the Radcliffe Observatory Quarter.

CONTEMPORARY AND DEVELOPING JERICHO

Walton Street and Little Clarendon Street come alive at night. They are leisure destinations for many from Oxford and wider afield. That will increase with the building of the Schwarzman Centre and concert hall.

The story of the Jericho mural from the creative influence James Salter.

"The mural was on the corner shop, formally a launderette, which is now the wine cafe on the corner of Walton Street and Little Clarendon street. It was derelict from 1996-2012 so in 2008 I decided to create the mural, to show all the shops and amenities what Jericho has to offer. I got in my good friend and artist Stuart Roper to paint the mural, which I then had enlarged onto canvas to fit all four boarded up windows of the now wine cafe.

It was enormous, and became known as the Jericho mural, and was a guide to all the wonder Jericho had to offer at the time. It was opened by the mayor and remained intact and untouched for over three years till the building was demolished and re-built. We also raised £1,000 which I donated to St Barnabas School".

The new Schwarzman Centre, costing £175 million and named after its American benefactor, will house a concert hall plus a theatre and the Humanities departments of the University, all brought together in one place.

St Paul's House, Lucy's Walton Street mixed use development.

'Greater Jericho'

Port Meadow and Little Clarendon Street - these two places, while not strictly within the Jericho Conservation Area are so close, influential and part of the overall picture that they are included for their interest.

Little Clarendon Street was once known as Black Boy Lane (after Charles II). It was later named Workhouse Lane, after the building formerly occupying today's Wellington Square; then, in the 1840s, Little Clarendon Street after the Earl of Clarendon (1609-1674). Little Clarendon Street was Oxford's 'Little Trendy Street' and in recent years has grown even more lively with new eateries, a specialist cheese shop and illuminations at night.

Street and bikes. The Oxford Wine Café. Gail's Bakery.

PORT MEADOW

The 'Lungs of Jericho'

This is the place known as Port Meadow. Tradition has it that it was granted to the Freemen of Oxford in the ninth century by King Alfred the Great in return for their support against the marauding Danes. In the Domesday book of 1086, it is written: 'All the burgesses of Oxford have pasture outside the walls in common, which pays six shillings and eight pence.' Since that day it has never been ploughed and never privately owned.

Generations have strolled here. Scholars and artists, naturalists and foragers, poets and pilgrims, stick-throwing dog walkers, lovers lost in the feeling of spaciousness… a timeless magic, the Meadow was also the site for the Sheriff of Oxford's (horse) races. And all this less than ten minutes walk from Jericho.

Cripley allotments and St Banabas Church from Willow Walk. A dawn skuller. Playtime on the frozen Meadow.

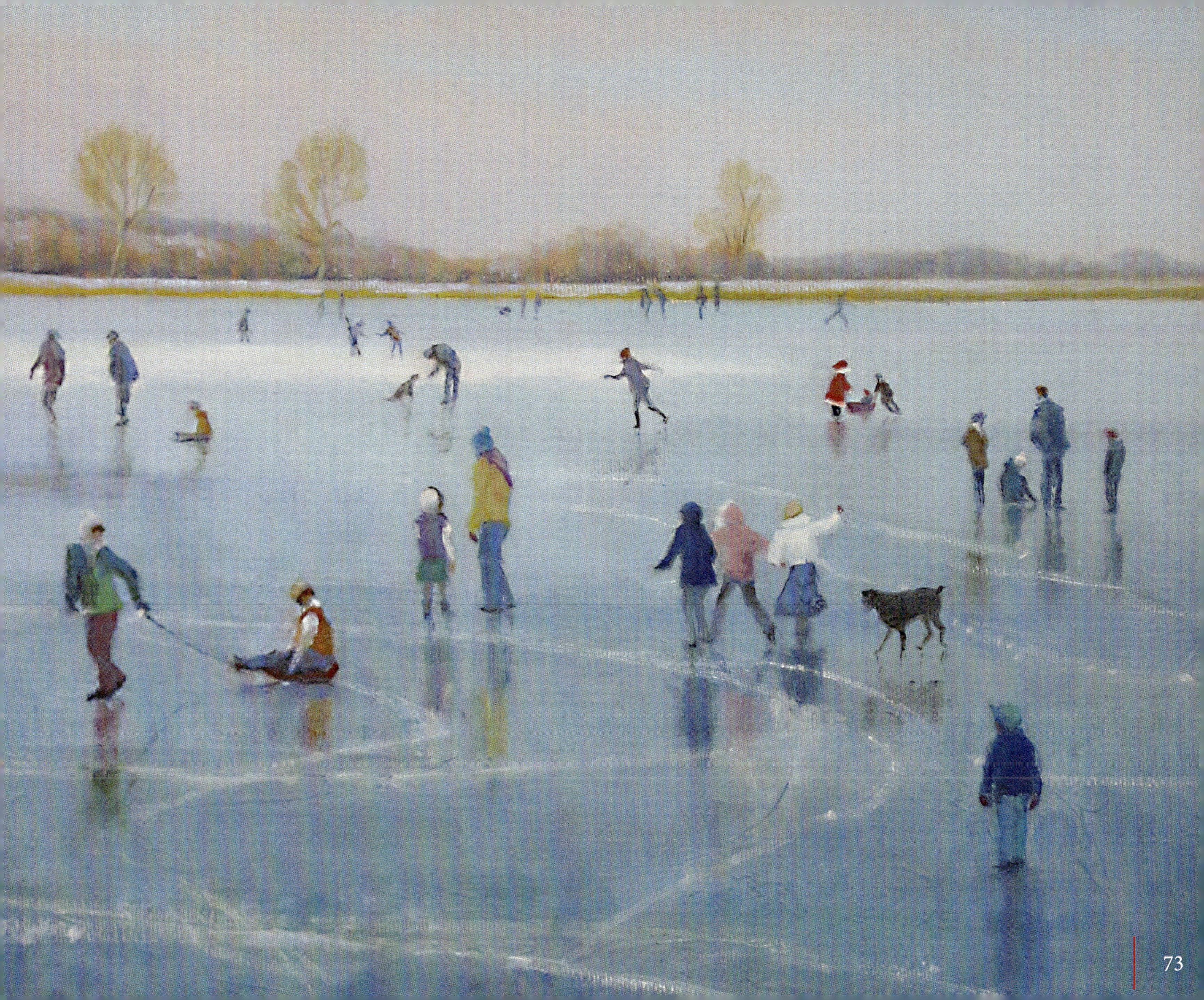

1. Lucy

Improving people's lives – sustainable homes, smart lighting and intelligent power.

@LUCY.GROUP | @LUCYGROUP | @LUCY_GROUP | LUCYGROUP.COM

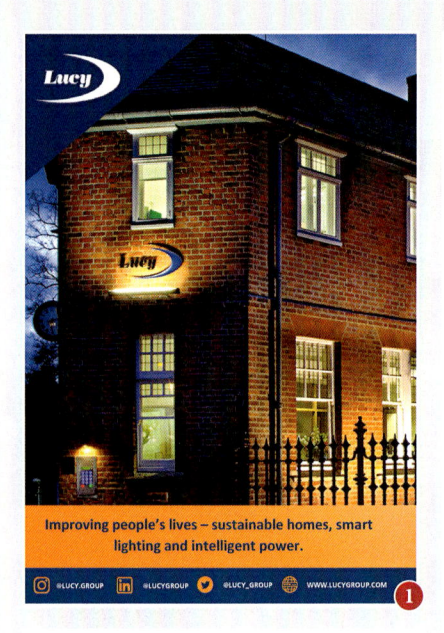

2. JERICHO Master Barbers

165 Kingston Road,
Oxford, OX2 6EG,

01865 576266

jericho.barbers.oxford@gmail.com
www.jerichobarbers.co.uk

We're a team of talented barbers located in Jericho, - dedicated to empowering men to look and feel fantastic, to give them the confidence to take on any situation in their stride. Whether it's important meetings, or social events, nights out, or your wedding we'll help you.

Make your social impact count.

3. LYNRACE MMXXI Lynrace Spirit of Walton Street Oxford

103 Walton Street
Oxford, OX2 6EB

01865 686156

spirit@lynrace.com
www.lynrace.com

Inspiring Creative Spirits
Cocktail bar, off-licence and venue. Independent home for contemporary spirits and cocktails.
A destination to try and share something special.
Open Wednesday to Saturday, 6pm to 11pm.

4. PAUL SOUTHOUSE ARCHITECTS

103 Walton Street
Oxford, OX2 6EB

01865 686108

studio@paulsouthouse.co.uk
www.paulsouthouse.co.uk

Inspiring Creative Design
Paul Southouse Architects is an innovative architectural practice working in and around Oxford, based in Jericho. We design and build bespoke homes and spaces, creating beauty and place.

St. Paul's House, Walton Street
(client: Lucy Group Ltd)

5. JERICHO GRILL

67 Walton Street,
Oxford, OX2 6AG

01865 559 668

info@jerichogrill.co.uk
www.jerichogrill.co.uk

Jericho Grill is an independent, contemporary grill and restaurant based in the heart of Jericho. We offer a wide range of delicious cuisine with daily specials, lunch and dinner menus.

6. BRANCA

109-111 Walton Street,
Oxford, OX2 6AJ

01865 807745

info@branca.co.uk
www.branca.co.uk

Opening over two decades ago, our modern restaurant, bar, cafe and destination deli offer bold flavours inspired by Italy, southern Europe and beyond. Our light-filled restaurant opens out onto a beautiful garden terrace and flexible dining spaces mean we can also host special occasions in our private party rooms. The deli counters are brimming with dishes cooked by our chefs, including our legendary focaccia and a dozen fresh salads daily.

7. KOTO Oxford

114 Walton Street,
Oxford, OX2 6AG

01865 553 000

kotorestaurantuk@gmail.com
www.kotorestaurant.co.uk

Koto Restaurant moved from North Parade to Jericho in 2020. Its authentic Japanese menu offers popular dishes including sushi, ramens and other familiar dishes both traditional and modern twists that are enjoyed in Japan. Koto is a fantastic location to enjoy Japanese beer, sake, whiskeys and teas for visitors and locals alike.
The friendly staff welcome both dine-in and 'to-go' customers during lunch and dinner hours.

8. JERICHO PHARMACY Your Health, Our Commitment

116 Walton St,
Oxford, OX2 6AJ

018656 557219

mail@jerichopharmacy.co.uk

Your health is our commitment
Jericho Pharmacy is an independent pharmacy at the heart of Jericho. The pharmacy recently re-opened under new management in May 2022 and serves the local area and beyond.

74

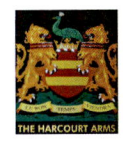

**Cranham Terrace,
Oxford, OX2 6DG**

01865 556669
www.harcourtarmsjericho.co.uk

The Harcourt Arms is Jericho's traditional local. It is the heart of the community, the pub that only serves drinks, along with regular live music. A secret courtyard garden is the perfect summer evening meeting spot. In winter, open fireplaces keep the welcome just as warm.

Featured in CAMRA's Good Beer Guide 2023.

Open daily from 5pm

❾

NOPS Property Letting

**47-48 Walton Street
Oxford, OX2 6AD**

01865 318538
post@northoxfordproperty.co.uk
www.nops.co.uk

North Oxford Property Services (NOPS) is a family run property letting agency in Jericho.

We manage and let over 1000 properties within the Oxford ring road, Jericho being our focus. Please ring Debbie 01865 318547 (direct) for a free consultation on the rental value of your property.

❿

ronapainting gallery

**34 Walton Street
Oxford, OX2 6AA**

info@ronapainting.com
www.ronapaintinggallery.com

Rona has been a painter for thirty years and has a sharp eye for quality. She wanted to create a permanent space where people can view and buy local work in person. She especially wants to support younger artists at the beginning of their career.

⓫

THE OXFORD WINE CAFÉ

**32 Little Clarendon Street
Oxford, OX1 2HU**

01865 604334
www.oxfordwinecafe.co.uk/

Our mission is to bring you the best wines from all over the world, made by smaller, ultra passionate boutique-style producers. We hope that you will find The Oxford Wine Café to be a small haven of quality where you can meet friends and enjoy the wines you want at a great price.

We host fun, informal events suitable for anyone - not just people who 'know about wine!'

⓬

CHRIS ANDREWS PUBLICATIONS

**13 Curtis Industrial Estate,
Oxford, OX2 0LX**

01865 723404
enquiries@cap-ox.com
www.cap-ox.com

Oxford-based publishers of calendars, diaries, guide books & tourist products featuring Oxford, the Cotswolds, Channel Islands and Belfast.

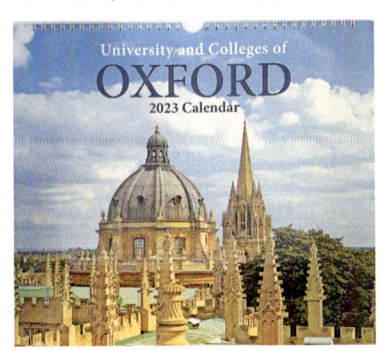

MY JERICHO

johnmair100@hotmail.com
www.myjericho.co.uk

MyJericho was set up in 2016 by John Mair and has since put on close to 300 events, talks, conversations, visits and more in and out of Jericho.

MyJericho events are held in-person at St Barnabas Church and virtually on YouTube. All talks can be found on myjericho.co.uk, where you can book your place at any event and make donations to keep MyJericho going.

75

LOCAL BUSINESSES

1. Lucy Group
2. Jericho Barbers
3. Lynrace Spirit
4. Paul Southouse Architects
5. Jericho Grill
6. Branca (Bar, Restaurant and Deli)
7. Koto
8. Jericho Pharmacy
9. Harcourt Arms
10. North Oxford Property Services
11. Rona Painting Gallery
12. The Oxford Wine Cafe

Walton Street

Map by Paul Southouse.

A FINAL VIEW

Dawn rowers with Jericho and
St Barnabas Church from
Port Meadow.

Acknowledgements

This book was initially made possible by generous donations from the Lucy Group, Towpath Productions/ Stuart Miller, Lynrace/Paul Southouse, Jericho Good Works/ John Mair and many smaller donations as well. The book was conceived and prepared by a small group of Jericho enthusiasts.

Chris Andrews has worked as a photographer and publisher in Oxford for over 40 years. His many books, calendars and cards may be seen in retail outlets locally and nationally.

Mark Davies is an Oxford local historian and guide, with a particular interest in Jericho, derived from living on a nearby residential narrowboat for nearly 30 years. His most relevant books are *A Towpath Walk in Oxford, Alice in Waterland, Stories of Oxford Castle,* and *Alice's Oxford on Foot.* He is the current chair of the Jericho Living Heritage Trust.

John Mair runs My Jericho(myjericho.co.uk) which is the events generator for the community. He has put on about three hundred Jericho live and virtual events in the last six years. John is a former BBC producer and the editor of 50 published books.

Paul Southouse is an architect and founder of Paul Southouse Architects (based on Walton Street, Jericho). The majority of the practice's work is in and around Oxford with many projects in Jericho itself - including the recent redevelopment of St Paul's House for Lucy Properties. Paul also owns and manages Lynrace Spirit - a bar, off-licence and venue for inspiring creative spirits.

Picture and Text Credits

In addition to those mentioned above and on Page 2,

The Publishers' are very grateful to artist Valerie Petts for permission to reproduce her paintings on the front cover and pps 7, 23, 28, 37, 39, 53, 55, 59, 72 and 73. Valerie, who has lived in Jericho since 1980 is an artist of international standing, with many books and publications to her name; her contribution is much appreciated. www.valeriepetts.co.uk

Page 31is gleaned mostly from *Oxford Pubs*, Dave Richardson (2015) and *An Encyclopaedia of Oxford Pubs, Inns and Taverns* Derek S. Honey (1998)

Port Meadow text: Courtesy of Tony Morris of https://morrisoxford.co.uk/